TAKING THE FLY.

THE BROOK TROUT

AND

THE DETERMINED ANGLER

A little pocket volume containing several descriptions of a fly fisher's paradise, and a few practical suggestions for the young angler

BY
CHARLES BARKER BRADFORD
AUTHOR OF "THE WILDFOWLERS," ETC.

NEW YORK
THE E. P. GROW PUBLISHING COMPANY
RICHMOND HILL, LONG ISLAND

COPYRIGHT, 1900,

BY

THE E. P. GROW PUBLISHING CO.

THE MERSHON COMPANY PRESS,
NO. 156 FIFTH AVENUE, NEW YORK, N.Y.

TO

J. CHARLES DAVIS

THESE LITTLE YARNS ARE DEDICATED IN REMEMBRANCE
OF SOME DELIGHTFUL DAYS PASSED IN HIS SO-
CIETY, AND IN GRATITUDE FOR AN
UNINTERRUPTED FRIENDSHIP
OF MANY YEARS.

. . . it carries us into the most wild and beautiful scenery of nature; amongst the mountain lakes, and the clear and lovely streams that gush from the higher ranges of elevated hills, or that make their way through the cavities of calcareous strata. How delightful in the early spring, after the dull and tedious time of winter, when the frosts disappear and the sunshine warms the earth and waters, to wander forth by some clear stream, to see the leaf bursting from the purple bud, to scent the odors of the bank perfumed by the violet, and enameled, as it were, with the primrose and the daisy; to wander upon the fresh turf below the shade of trees, whose bright blossoms are filled with the music of the bee; and on the surface of the waters to view the gaudy flies sparkling like animated gems in the sunbeams, whilst the bright and beautiful trout is watching them from below; to hear the twittering of the water-birds, who, alarmed at your approach, rapidly hide themselves beneath the flowers and leaves of the water-lily; and as the season advances, to find all these objects changed for others of the same kind, but better and brighter, till the swallow and the trout contend as it were for the gaudy May fly, and till in pursuing your amusement in the calm and balmy evening, you are serenaded by the songs of the cheerful thrush . . . performing the offices of paternal love, in thickets ornamented with the rose and woodbine.—*Days of Fly Fishing, 1828.*

"Gentlemen, let not prejudice prepossess you. I confess my discourse is like to prove suitable to my recreation, calm and quiet. . . And so much for the prologue of what I mean to say."

Izaak Walton.

AUTHOR'S ACKNOWLEDGMENTS.

THE article, "Fly Fishing for Trout," I contributed in its original form to *Sports Afield*, Mr. Claude King's Western journal.

The article "Trout and Trouting," as I originally prepared it, was entitled "Near-by Trout Streams," and was written for and published in *Outing*, when I was field editor of that delightful magazine.

"Trouting in Canadensis Valley" is rewritten from a little story of mine penned for the noted angler and ichthyologist, Mr. William C. Harris, and published by him in *The American Angler*.

And most of the items in "Little Casts" are from a collection of paragraphs I have contributed to the New York *Herald* and various sporting periodicals in the past dozen years.

For the little pen-and-ink sketches I am indebted to our jovial artist, Leppert.

The picture, "Taking the Fly," is a reproduction from an etching in my possession, presented to me by Mr. William M. Carey, whose etchings and paintings in oil are well known to American sportsmen.

"The Fly Rod's Victim" is reproduced from a

photograph framed in birch bark and presented to me by the poet, Isaac McLellan.

"The Brook Trout" illustration is from a photograph of a captive specimen in an aquarium, the engraving being loaned me by Mr. John P. Burkhard, publisher of *Field and Stream*.

RICHMOND HILL,
 Long Island, N. Y.,
May 1, 1900.

FLY FISHING FOR TROUT.

The variety of rivers require different ways of angling.—The Complete Angler.

HE art of catching fishes with artificial lures in imitation of natural insects is the most chivalric of all methods of angling.

Fishes, particularly trout, often hook themselves when they seize the fly of a fisherman using a pliant rod that will yield and spring freely. As the game strikes, the angler strikes, hooking the fish swiftly but delicately by a simple turn of the wrist. The trout is not flaunted up in the air by force, as some coarse perch fishermen lift their catch. The trout fisher does not use his arm at all in hooking a trout, beyond aiding the hand in holding the rod for the wrist to do the work. A practiced troutman can secure his fish by moving his hand five inches—a little backward nervous twist of the wrist.

Trout often snap a fly and spit it out so quickly that the tyro does not have a chance to strike and hook the prize. At other times they take hold more slowly, and afford the beginner more opportunity to hook them, and, as I have said, they very often hook themselves.

The beginner will have some trouble in overcoming the excitement or "trout fever" that always accompanies the trout's rise and strike, but experience will gradually make him more calm and active at this important moment. The tyro trout fisher is often more frightened at the rise of the trout than he would be at the flush of a noisy grouse or the springing of a surprised deer.

When you have hooked the fish, always handle him as if he were but lightly secured. Do not attempt to lift him out or yank him up to you. Keep the line gently taut, and softly lead the prize out of rough water or away from stones, grasses, logs, or tree branches. Do not let him come to the surface until he is pretty well exhausted and you are about to put him in the landing-net. If he is a large fish, tow him ashore if the water edge will permit. Where there are overhanging banks this cannot be done. Do not be in a hurry to get him out of the water. Be calm and work carefully.

If the fish is large enough to overcome the reel click and run off the line, let him do so, but check him and guide him according to any obstruction there may be.

When he has rushed here and there for some little time with his mouth open and with a constant check—the line should always be taut—he will become tired, and when he is tired he will not rush. Then softly reel him in, being careful not to let him come in contact with a stone or weed, which is sure to arouse him again. Reel him up until your leader touches the tip of the rod. Then, if the leader is of the correct length and if the rod is properly pliant, he will be near enough for you to put your landing-net under him, tail first, as all fish should be netted. Do this quickly, without making a splashing swoop, and he will soon grace your creel.

Several persons have expressed an objection to a list of flies I once named in *Sports Afield,* saying a good angler might kill just as many trout on quarter the number.

Any angler can take even less than one-quarter of the enumerated list and catch fully as many brook trout as one who might use all of the flies mentioned—if he can pick out the ones the trout are rising to without trying them all until he discovers the killing ones. A chef might please his master with one or two of the forty courses billed, if he knew what the man wanted. Sometimes an angler can judge the appropriate fly to use by observing nature in seeing trout rise to the live fly; but there are times when trout are not rising, times when they are tired of the fly upon the water, and times when the real fly is not on the wing. Then the angler is expected to take matters in his own hands and whip about quietly until he discovers the proper thing. It is better to try for the right ones with a list of twenty-nine than whip over a list of a thousand or more. I have learned from experience that trout, like human beings,

THE TROUT BROOK.

are in love with a variety of foods at different times. Their tastes change with the months, the weeks, the days, the hours, and, under certain conditions which I will presently explain, the minutes. When I mention twenty-nine different patterns as being seasonable at a stated period, I do not mean to say that the trout will rise to them all and at any time and under all conditions. In the first place, the person using them might be a tyro unfamiliar with the gentle art, the streams might be dried up, there might be an earthquake, the flies might be too large, too coarse, and for that matter a thousand other conditions might interfere. I fish dozens of streams in different localities several times every month during the legal season, and I have been a fond angler—if not a skillful one—since my tenth birthday. Experience on the streams, a true love for nature, and a careful attention to my notebook enable me to separate the artificial flies into monthly lists. No man can class them into weekly or daily lots.

The " Eastern gentleman who said if

he could have but one fly he would take a yellow one," is probably a good angler, for a yellow fly is a fair choice. If I could have but one fly I should take a—ah! I cannot name its color; 'tis the quaker, a cream, buff, grayish honey-yellow shade.

Trout change in their tastes by the month, week, day, hour, and minute. There are flies among the list given for this or that month that they will not rise to to-day or perhaps to-morrow, but surely there are some among the list that will please them, and you have to discover those particular ones, and so, as I have said before, 'tis better to search among twenty-nine than twenty-nine hundred.

In July of a certain season I waded a stream in Pennsylvania and had these flies with me: Quaker, Oak, Codun, Reuben Wood, White Miller, Yellow Sallie, Hare's Ear, Iron Dun, Brown Palmer, Cahill, and a few others. The first day I killed eighteen trout in fishing fifty yards in a small stream running partly through a large open field and partly through bushes, fishing from the left bank. Twelve were taken on a brown palmer, four on a dark-gray midge, and two on a tiny yellow-gold-brown fly. I fished three hours, in which time I received exactly two hundred and fifteen strikes; eighteen, as I have said, proved killing. I fished stealthily up and down the stream, hiding here and there and making the most difficult of casts at all times. I went up and down the little stream a half dozen times, never going into the wood, but merely fishing from where the stream came out of the wood to where it hid itself again beyond the field. Part of the water I fished, as I say, was in underbush, but I did not leave the field.

Now I am going to show you how the tastes of trout varied by minutes, in two instances at least, and I desire you to know every little detail. To well convince you that the casts I made were difficult, I will say that my line became fastened in twigs, leaves, and bushes every other toss. I had to put the flies through little openings no larger than the creel head and take chances of getting the leader caught while on the way, and after it was there and on its return. I sometimes whipped twenty times at a little pool before I reached it. There were logs, branches, mosses, cresses, leaves, and grasses to avoid. The water in parts was swift and still, narrow, shallow, and deep, sometimes being four feet wide and three feet deep, and then ten feet wide and three inches deep; sometimes running smartly over bright grasses or pebbles and light in color, and in other places lying dark and still in pools made by logs and deep holes.

A tyro would have fished the ground in ten minutes and caught nothing; some anglers would have gone over it once in twenty-five minutes and taken a half dozen fish. I had the day to myself; I had nowhere else to go; I was out for sport, recreation, and study,—not fish, for I am a lover of nature in general,—and so I took three hours at the play, and fished and observed inch by inch like a mink, the king of trouters.

I say I had two hundred and fifteen

strikes, out of which I killed eighteen trout, and you are surprised. You think you could have done better, much better, but I know you could not—you could not have done as well as I did and I wish that I could put you to a test. I have seen a *fontinalis* rise to a small coachman twenty-six times, snapping apparently at the feather each time, but never allowing himself to be hooked nor hooking himself. He was playing. He was a young trout, but an educated one, and well knew there was no danger if he kept his wits about him. I have witnesses to this performance who will substantiate my story, and I can easily further prove the truthfulness of the statement by taking you to a stream where a similar performance may be enacted. And I have seen an uneducated trout rise and snap at a fly without taking it. The first one rose in play, this one in curiosity—and there are trout that will rise in anger. All of them may know the bait is not food. It is a mistake to think that all brook trout will spurt from a fly the very second they discover it is not real food, as it is an error to believe that all brook trout will take the fly when they know it is the living thing. All trout are not alike; they vary in their tastes and antics as they do in color and size. Mind you, I speak only of one species here—the true brook trout, *salvelinus fontinalis*, and thus the material should be interesting. The day I took my creel of eighteen was a fair one; we had rain the day before; the water was clear and the stream was in ordinary condition. The brown hackle which killed twelve of the eighteen was on a No. 8 hook; the other two flies were tied on No. 16, as the hackle should have been, for the fish were small and the stream was in a small-fly condition and quite right for the daintiest leaders and the finest midges. But the hackle seemed to please the trout; all sizes appeared to jump at it. I hooked many that were not over three inches long! Several times when taking my flies from the water for a new cast, I lifted a poor little trout up in the air back of me, like the scurvy fisherman who makes a practice of landing all his fish by yanking them out.

So you see it pays to be patient on the stream and try all sorts of gentle tricks with *fontinalis*. You must not hurry; you must not be coarse; you must not be careless and untidy with your fly-book. Take your time, fish slowly, surely, and delicately. Be not weary of the play: banish the thought of discouragement, keep at the sport for sport alone, and study as you angle.

A little trout will rise to a fly he has missed one or more times; a large trout will seldom do so. When you miss a big trout do not give him back the fly for ten minutes, and then if you miss him again, change the pattern, wait a little while, and he is once more ready for the rise—if the new fly suits him.

I never raised a trout on the scarlet ibis fly. I believe it is a poor color on the well-fished waters, just as I believe that all flies are killing on wild streams. New trout will take old flies; old trout love new ones and many old ones. Personally I like the sober colors in flies for all seasons on all water, though I well appreciate the old rule: "When the day is bright and where the water is clear, small flies and plain colors; in deep and dull waters and on dark days and in the evening the brighter and larger ones." Trout do not in all cases show their liking to flies in accordance with any condition of weather or water, though as a rule it is advisable to use lighter colors when the day and water are dull, which is not saying, however, that fish will not rise to loud flies on bright days or sober flies in dull weather, for the tastes of trout vary like the tastes of other living things, and nothing can equal them in erraticness when fly-feeding.

You must give *fontinalis* sport, for he very often strikes for play more than food, and, like every other living thing, loves a choice of variety.

There is an old story that if the angler's book has a pattern of fly in exact imitation of the real fly upon the trout water, he has but to join it as the stretcher to fill his creel. Ogden tells us in so many words: "Give not the trout an exact imitation of the real fly upon the water, for your artificial fly will then be one in a thousand. Something startling will please them better—loud gold body, strange-colored wings—and an odd fellow may take it for sport if nothing else."

While this is a good bit of advice, it does not seem right to me to send it forth in such a sweeping manner. The question of whether we should imitate nature in general fly building has long been in vogue. Some say we should do so, and others that it does not matter. Both are correct—there are times when we should copy the living flies, and times when we should use those artificial things that have no resemblance to nature's insects. I have come upon a water where the trout were rising to the small dusky miller, and have, by putting on the artificial fly of this order, taken a dozen beauties in good play. It was because I arrived just in time; the trout were not tired of their course. Perhaps twenty minutes later they would not have done more than eyed my cast. In that case, even if the water were covered with a species of the real fly, it would have been better to have flailed something different. Copy nature if the fish be devouring—not alone because the fly is on the water; they may be tired of it. Sometimes there are flies being taken that are not seen by the angler, for trout can snap a fly upon the wing. Fly-fishing is not an easy pursuit; 'tis a real science. Rules are good, but we must not fail to suit the rules to conditions.

No; you are not supposed to use the entire list, for to-day the trout may not favor over two or three of them; to-morrow he may take six of them—all different from those he may show a liking for to-day. It is all very well for an angler to take but three dozen coachmen and brown and gray hackle for the Western trout (or any trout that is not educated up to the standard of the trout that is fished for incessantly), but I should not like to make a month's trouting trip and take along only three kinds of flies, even if I had dozens of each of the three and if my favorite quaker were one of the trio, no matter where the stream—East, West, North, or South.

Some days after my catch of eighteen I visited the field again and fished from the point where the stream entered the wood down to a beautiful little waterfall. I took twenty-one of fair size—one on a yellow Sallie, one on an oak fly, four on an Esquimaux dun, five on a hare's ear, and nine on the quaker. This day I had ninety-three rises—not as many as on the day I took the eighteen and had two hundred and fifteen rises. The day was dark, the water very clear and shallow, and there had been no rain for ten days.

This was the occasion of learning more about striking the Eastern brook trout than I had ever before enjoyed. The old rule is to strike on the second of the rise, and, while I do not think this electric quickness should be practiced in all cases and under all conditions, I found it was the rule this day, especially in the one deep pool I found. In other places —one in particular, where I saw six of my catch make every move in taking the flies—I found it necessary to depart from the old rule and strike not upon the second of the rise. I very often gave wrist too quickly. It all goes to prove that rules are not to be exercised at all times and under all conditions. We must make allowances. I came upon one quiet piece of water that was as clear and still as glass; I could see every detail of the pebbles at the bottom. Eight pretty trout were in this bed of silent water, resting without a perceptible movement —not even that delicate wave of the tail so common with the trout in his balancing in running water. They did not see me; a bush hid my form. When my slender rod-tip moved over the water and the leader with the flies went down gently upon the surface, the trout thought (all animals think) the wind had stirred the frail branch of an adjacent tree and swept into the water upon a cobweb three insects for their feeding. Four rushed for the deceit and two were hooked quietly and quickly. I landed them and went away to return to the same spot a half hour later. Seven trout were there this time. I flailed gently over them, but received no rushing rise; one little fellow came up deliberately, broke water

A GOOD CAMPING GROUND.

two inches behind the little dun, and then returned to his old position. Then two others did precisely the same as their companion had done, excepting that one chose the oak fly for his inspection. Then they sank themselves, and a fourth gamester spurted up to the dun and took it in his mouth much as a sunfish would suck in a bit of worm. I struck him, and he made a splash that nearly drove a near-by-perched catbird into hysterics, and sent the other trout up, down, and across the stream like so many black streaks of lightning. Now, had I flailed at these fish from above or below, and not just over them, where I saw every move they made, I should have given them wrist on the second of their rise—as I did in the case of the first two that made the first rush—and lost any chance of success.

No, I say, we must not always follow rules regardless of conditions. We must not judge all trout alike, even if they be of one species. Men, though of one race, are not all alike in their habits any more than they are in their sizes and colors.

I found in some parts of the stream that as long as I changed the flies I had rises; in other parts no trout took the fly, no matter how I worked it. Perhaps there were no fish hereabout; perhaps they saw me; perhaps they were not hungry, and perhaps there were hundreds and thousands of other reasons why they were not to be taken in these certain places.

No man can strictly follow rules in all cases and take trout upon every occasion of his trials. Conditions govern, and must be studied—conditions, conditions.

TROUT TRUTHS.

D. W. C. FARRINGTON.

> I live not in myself, but I become
> Portion of that around me; and to me
> High mountains are a feeling, but the hum
> Of human cities torture.
> —BYRON.

HAT is the best season of the year to go a-fishing?

I think the best time is when you feel like it and can leave home and business. The desire for fishing is like some diseases, in attacking a man with great severity without notice. It can be no more resisted than falling in love can be resisted, and, like love, the best treatment is its gratification.

What is the best time o' day for fishing?

Any time after breakfast. Never go before, for trout are not early risers. I have known men to get out of bed at daylight, making much noise, to the disgust of those who wished to sleep, and rush off with an empty stomach save perhaps for a drink of whisky, and return several hours later to a cold breakfast, having captured nothing but a headache. Trout will bite just when they feel like it, and the best way to ascertain their biting time is to give them a frequent opportunity.

How about the wind and the weather?

Trout will bite when the wind blows and when it does not. A cloudy day is best except when they rise better on a bright, sunny one. They also often bite well when it rains.

What fly is best?

The fly the trout seem to fancy most on the day you are out. I never go without at least fifty varieties. You may as well ask a woman what style of bonnet she prefers. The taste of trout and women is governed by a similar law, and they change it quite as often. I once made a fly that was so ugly that it frightened my cat out of the room, and yet it proved a great killer. The surest way is to have every known specimen, and to try them all.

What kind of hook is best?

The one with a sharp point, and when you miss a trout charge your clumsiness to the hook and say you prefer some other make.

As conditions are innumerable, it is difficult to make rules to-day which will not fail to-morrow. My advice is—go often and visit many localities. Kill no more fish than you require for your own eating, and do that in the most scientific manner. A trout is a gentleman, and should be treated as such and lured with only delicate and humane weapons.

TROUT AND TROUTING.

A day with not too bright a beam ;
A warm, but not a scorching, sun.
—CHARLES COTTON.

HERE can I enjoy trout fishing amid good scenery and good cheer without its necessitating a lengthy absence from the city? That is a question which frequently rises in the mind of the toilers in the busy centers of the East, and it is one becoming daily more difficult to answer. Yet there are still nearby trout streams where a creel of from fifteen to fifty, or even more, in favorable weather, might be made. One such locality, which for years local sportsmen have proven, lies within a four hours' ride of either Philadelphia or New York. All that is necessary is to take the railroad, which conveys you to Cresco, in Monroe County, Pa., and a ride or drive of five miles

through the Pocono Mountains will land you in the little village of Canadensis, in the valley of the Brodhead; and within the radius of a few miles on either side fully a dozen other unposted streams ripple along in their natural state, not boarded, bridged, dammed, or fenced by the hand of man, thanks to the naturally uncultivatable condition of the greater part of this paradise for trout fishers. The villagers of Canadensis do their trading and receive their mail at Cresco, and it is an easy matter to obtain excellent food and lodgings for a dollar a day at one of the many farmhouses dotting here and there the valleys, and a seat when needful in one of the several private conveyances running every day between the two villages.

The open season for trout in Pennsylvania is from April 15 until July 15, and there appears to be no particularly favored period during these three months, for the trout here afford sport equally well at all times, though they greatly vary in their tastes for the fly.

If one goes there in the early part of the

open season, when the weather is cold, he should engage a room and take his meals at the farmhouse selected; but if the trip is made in the early part of June or any time after that, during the open season, camp life may be enjoyed with great comfort.

Two favorite waters within walking distance from any of the farmhouses in Canadensis are Stony Run and the Buckhill. The great Brodhead, a famous old water in the days of Thaddeus Norris, and noted then and now for its big trout, flows in the valley proper, within a stone's throw of the farmhouse at which I engaged quarters. Spruce Cabin Run, a mile distant, is a charming stream, but the trout here are not very large beyond the deep pools at the foot of Spruce Falls and in the water flowing through Turner's fields and woods above the falls.

Any of these streams will afford plenty of sport, but if one wishes to visit a still more wild, romantic, and beautiful trout water, he has only to walk a little farther or take a buckboard wagon and ride to the mighty Bushkill, a stream that must not be confounded with the Buckhill, which lies in an opposite direction from Canadensis.

The Bushkill is the wildest stream in the region, and is fished less than any of the others named, one reason being that there are plenty of trout in the waters of Canadensis, which can be fished without one going so far. For those who like to camp, the Bushkill is the proper locality. I spent a day there with friends one season, and we caught in less than two hours, in the liveliest possible manner, all the trout five of us could eat throughout the day, and four dozen extra large ones which we took home to send to friends in the city.

"The trout in the Bushkill," remarked one of my companions, "are so wild that they're tame." An expression based upon the greediness and utter disregard of the enemy with which *fontinalis*, in his unfamiliarity with man, took the fly. I remember having a number of rises within two feet of my legs as I was taking in my line for a front toss.

I know men who have many times

traveled a thousand miles from New York on an angling trip to different famous waters who have not found either the sport or the scenery to be enjoyed on the Bushkill.

The lower Brodhead below the point at which this stream and Spruce Cabin Run come together is very beautiful. It is owned by a farmer who lives on its banks, and who has never been known to refuse anglers permission to fish there when they asked for the privilege.

There are four natural features in the scenery about Canadensis that are especially prized by the countrymen there— the Sand Spring, Buckhill Falls, Spruce Cabin Falls and the Bushkill Falls.

The Sand Spring is so called because grains of brilliant sand spring up with the water. This sand resembles a mixture of gold and silver dust; it forms in little clouds just under the water's bubble and then settles down to form and rise again and again. This effect, with the rich colors of wild pink roses, tiny yellow watercups, blue lilies, and three shades of green in the cresses and deer tongue that grow all about, produces, indeed, a pretty picture. The spring is not over a foot in diameter, but the sand edges and the pool cover several feet.

Being located at one side of the old road between Cresco and Canadensis every visitor has an opportunity of seeing it without going more than a few feet out of his direct way. Some of the stories told about the old sand spring are worth hearing, and no one can tell them better or with more special pleasure than the farmers living thereabout. One man affirms that "more 'an a hundred b'ar and as many deer have been killed while drinking the crystal water of the spring."

Each of the falls is a picture of true wild scenery. Though some miles apart they may be here described in the same paragraph.

Great trees have fallen over the water from the banks and lodged on huge projecting moss-covered rocks; they are additional obstacles to the rushing, roaring, down-pouring water, which flows through and over them like melted silver. This against the dark background of the mountain woods, the blue and snow-white of the heavens, the green of the rhododendron-lined banks and the streams' bottoms of all-colored stones creates a series of charming and ever-varying views.

A half dozen trout, weighing from one to two pounds and a half, may always be seen about the huge rock at the point where lower Brodhead and the Spruce Cabin Run come together, and hundreds may be seen in the stream below the Buckhill Falls. I do not know that fish may be actually seen in any other parts of the waters of Canadensis, but at these points the water is calm and the bottom smooth, and the specimens are plainly in view.

Do not waste time on the "flock" lying about the big rock at Brodhead Point. The trout there will deceive you. I played with them a half day, and before I began work on them I felt certain I would have them in my creel in a half hour's time. They are a pack of pampered idlers who do not have to move a fin to feed. All the trout food comes

" . . . Down-pouring water . . . like melted silver."

rushing down both streams from behind these big rocks into the silent water and floats right up to the very noses of these gentlemen of leisure. If you have any practicing to do with the rod and fly do it here. These trout are very obliging; they will lie there all day and enjoy your casting all sorts of things at them. This is a good place to prove to yourself whether you are a patient fisherman or not.

And now a few words about the proper tackle for mountain streams. Most anglers use rods that are too heavy and too long. During my first visit I used a rod rod of eight feet, four ounces, and I soon found that, while it was a nice weight, it was too long for real convenience, although there were rods used there nine and ten feet long. My rod was the lightest and one of the shortest ever seen in the valley. There are only a few open spots where long casts are necessary, and a long, ordinary-weight trout rod is of very little service compared with one of seven, seven-and-a-half, or eight feet, four or three ounces, that can be handled well along the narrow, bush-lined, tree-branch-covered streams.

The greater part of the fishing is done by sneaking along under cover of the rocks, logs, bushes, and the low-hanging branches, as casts are made in every little pool and eddy. I use a lancewood rod, but of course the higher-priced popular split bamboo is just as good. I shall not claim my rod's material is the better of the two, as some men do when speaking of their tackle, but I am quite sure I shall never say the split bamboo is more than its equal. I do not advise as to the material; I speak only of the weight and length. Let every man use his choice, but I seriously advise him to avoid the cheap-priced split bamboo rod.

If split bamboo is the choice, let it be the work of a practical rod-maker. Any ordinary wood rod is better than the four-dollar split bamboo affair.

The leader should be of single gut, but the length should be a trifle more than is commonly used. Twelve feet is my favorite amount. The reel should be the lightest common click reel. The creel, a willow one that sells for a dollar in the stores; and the flies—here's the rub—must be the smallest and finest in the market. Large, cheap, coarse flies will never do for Eastern waters, and you must not fail to secure your list of the proper kind, as well as all your outfit, before you start on your trip. The only decent thing on sale in the village stores is tobacco.

When you buy your flies buy lots of them, for, be you a tyro or practical angler, you will lose them easier on these streams than you imagine. Yes, you must be very careful about the selection of your flies. They must be small and finely made, high-priced goods. I wish I might tell you who to have make them, but I dare not, lest I be charged with advertising a particular house. Regarding the patterns to use, I will say that none are more killing than the general list, if they are the best made and used according to the old rule all are familiar with—dark colors on cold days and bright ones on warm days. The later the season the louder the fly—that is, when the season closes during hot weather, as it does in Canadensis. My favorite time here is from June 15 to July 15, the closing day, but any time after the first two weeks of the open season is very charming. I avoid the first week or two because the weather is then cold and the trout are more fond of natural bait than the artificial fly. Men take hundreds of fish early in the season with worms and minnows.

I never wear rubber boots to wade in. An old pair of heavy-soled shoes with spikes in their bottoms, and small slits cut in the sides to let the water in and out, and a pair of heavy woolen socks comprise my wading footwear. The slits must not be large enough to let in coarse sand and pebbles, but I find it absolutely necessary to have a slight opening, for if there be no means for the water to run freely in and out, the shoes fill from the tops and become heavy. Rubber boots are too hot for my feet and legs, while the water is never too cold. I have often had wet feet all day, and have never yet experienced any ill effects from it.

I never use a staff in wading, but I should, for here in some places it is very hard to wade. I have often fallen down in water up to my waist, overbalanced by the heavy current, where the bottoms were rough, with sharp, slimy stones. If you carry a staff, follow the custom of the old anglers and tie it to your body with a string to keep it out of the way and allow your hands to be as free as possible for a strike. Your landing-net should be a small one, minus any metal, with a foot and a half handle, and a string tied to a front button on your garment should allow it to be slung over your shoulder onto your back when not in use.

Of course, these little points about the use of different things are all familiar to the angler with but the slightest experience, and will appear to him neither instructive nor interesting, but we must, as gentle anglers, give a thought or two to the earnest tyro, for we were young once ourselves.

I always carry two fly books with me; one big fellow with the general fly stock in, which is kept at the farmhouse, and a little one holding two dozen flies and a dozen leaders, which I carry on the stream. A string tied to this, too, will prevent the unpleasantness of having it fall in the water and glide away from you. I even tie a string to my pipe and knife. The outing hat is an important thing to me. Mine is always a soft brown or gray felt, and I use it to sit on in damp and hard places fifty times a day.

TROUTING IN CANADENSIS VALLEY.

THIS is a *fontinalis* paradise. With my friend George Blake, I creeled the little heroes by the dozen every day for a week. We each could have easily caught fifty in an afternoon had we cared to do so, but there were other rural pleasures to attend to, and we were not dealing in fish, and saw more beauty in just enough to eat than in an unnecessary quantity. Fishermen are generally known as "stretchers," and I do not deny that they do sometimes resort to an innocent little fib when a yarn may amuse many and injure no one, but I must say that this country's beauties are too numerous to overpraise by all the exaggeration of all the liars in the world. No word of mouth or pen could do justice to nature in these mountains. And I need not elaborate about the fish; the truth is strong enough.

Brook trout weighing a quarter of a pound to a pound and a half are taken every day by anglers, who more than fill their creels. Milton D. Price and Mathias Ellenberg took in one day sixty-five beauties on the stream known as Stony Run, and Wesley J. Price and a gentleman from Philadelphia took half a hundred the day before above the Buckhill Falls. Another great stream in this region is the Bushkill, and still another is Brodhead's Creek. The latter flows past our cabin, and is famous for big trout. My favorite is Spruce Cabin Stream, above and below the beautiful Spruce Cabin Falls. There are big trout in this water, especially at the bottom of the falls, and I can—if I will—take fifty trout in an afternoon, and they'll weigh from a quarter of a pound to one pound and a half. I like something besides fish about a stream, and this is why I am fond of the Spruce Cabin water.

There are not many anglers in love with the place. Though beautiful, it is very hard to fish. I have to creep under great trees that have fallen over the water and then wade up to my waist to gain certain points in order to get along down the stream. The banks are lined with trees and shrubbery, and my line is ever getting tangled. One does not need to be a fly-casting-tournament angler to fish any of the Canadensis waters. Distance in the cast is not required as much as accuracy at more than one or two places on each stream. The rest of the fishing is done by short, low casts, and by creeping under branches and letting the line float with the ripples into the eddies. Every step or two there are little falls, and in the white, bubbling water at their bottom a trout may be taken. Under the big fall, and in the still waters above and below, the big trout hide.

Artificial flies are the popular bait with the gentle angler, though all sizes of trout will take worms, and the big, educated trout like minnows. Both small, medium, and large trout like flies if the flies are the right kind. We have had great trouble in getting good flies. I brought four dozen with me, and not over a half dozen of them are worth the gut tied to them; they are of coarse material, and bad in color. The six decent ones are the work of an artist. I could give his name, but it might look like an advertisement and spoil my yarn. Trout like choice food just as much as human beings. You may stick an oyster shell on a reed and decoy a summer yellow leg, but you can't hook a trout on any kind of a fly. They know a thing or two.

Tyros who angle in a trout country without success go home and say there are no trout. They don't think about conditions of water and weather; about their line lighting in the water before their bait; about their coarse line and poor flies.

Trout are philosophers, not only the educated ones, those which have been hooked and seen others hooked, but trout in general. They're born that way. A young man came up here the other day with an old cane pole, weighing fully three pounds, and a big salt water sinker, and he went away saying there were few trout in these waters. I think he had a float with him, too, but am not sure.

A word or two about appropriate tackle for mountain streams, and I'll put up the pen and joint the rod again. In the city a few weeks ago I proudly displayed a four-ounce, nine-foot lancewood rod, and my friends laughed at me, saying it was too frail for any service. Now, I find this rod, shortened two feet, just the thing for this country where trout run small and where there's no long casting. I frequently run across good anglers here with five-ounce rods, and have seen two four-ounce rods. There is no use for a rod above four ounces in weight and seven feet in length. When I come again I shall use a three-ounce rod. The reel should be the lightest and smallest common click, and the line the finest enameled silk. The flies—here's the main thing—should be the best, and of the smallest brook trout pattern. Next year, when I make up my supply, I'll pack fully two hundred, and they'll be the best. The dearest-priced flies are none too good.

Oh, I must say a word about trout eating before I close. I've tried them in all styles, and the best way, I think, is when they're roasted over a camp fire on a little crotch stick, one prong in the head and the other in the tail. And the worst way, I think, is when they're fried in a pan with bad butter or poor lard.

Blake and I are in our glory. Our only displeasure is in knowing that our perspiring city friends are not as comfortable. The days here are warm and bright—not hot and close—and the nights cool and clear, so that we live merrily all the time.

I went about five blocks down the stream in front of the cabin to two great boulders, one morning, and there, during a little sun shower, took a *salvelinus fontinalis* that weighed just a little over two pounds and a quarter. He rose to a pinkish, cream-colored fly, with little brown spots on the wings. I forget its name, but it's one of the six really good ones I referred to. Milton Price was with me at the capture, and we decided to keep the fish alive, so I took off one of the cords tied about my trousers at the bot-

THE BROOK TROUT—SALVELINUS FONTINALIS.

toms (I never wear wading boots in warm weather), put it through his gill, and tied the other end to a submerged tree-root. Then Milton kept guard while I ran to the cabin for a big pail, and then Mr. Trout was lodged in a small box, with bars tacked over the top, and placed under a spout running from the old mill race. He was a big specimen—large enough to saddle and ride to town, the cook said. And pretty—as pretty as a bunch of lilacs and giant ferns decked with winter green berries.

IN THE POCONO MOUNTAINS.

RICHARD J. A. PASTERNACK.

'Twas an employment for his idle time, which was then not idly spent, for angling was, after tedious study, a rest to his mind, a cheerer of his spirits, a diverter of sadness, a calmer of unquiet thoughts, a moderator of passions, a procurer of contentedness, and it begat habits of peace and patience in those that professed and practiced it.—*Izaak Walton.*

MADE a trip to Canadensis, Pennsylvania, in April, for a few days' trout fishing. Canadensis is in Monroe County, in the Pocono Mountains. The nearest railroad station is at Cresco, on the Delaware, Lackawanna, and Western R. R. Cresco is one hundred and ten miles from New York. I found first-class accommodations at Brookside Cottage, in the Canadensis Valley. D. M. Crane is the

proprietor, and he furnishes everything in the way of fishing supplies, bait, etc.

There are seven or eight very good trout streams in the vicinity, Stony Run being the best. Goose Pond Run, Spruce Cabin, Buckhill Run, Brodhead Run and Bushkill Run are also very good. The trout caught in Stony Run were from eight to sixteen and eighteen inches in length. In Brodhead Run they run from eight to ten or twelve, as a rule, although I caught an eighteen-inch specimen there.

The first day's fishing at Brodhead Run brought me a nice mess of trout, and the second day at Stony Run I had excellent play.

With a party I drove over to Bushkill Run, which is eight miles from Canadensis, but here found the water too high for fishing. The snow was still on the mountains, but melting rapidly, and this was probably the cause of the stream being so high.

Mr. Crane informs me that fine bear and deer hunting and grouse and hare shooting may be had in the autumn and winter. There is excellent duck shooting at Goose Pond, and also good pike fishing there.

I consider this one of the best places in the country for fishing, hunting, and camping. The water is excellent for wading. The streams are romantic and wild, and one can walk miles without seeing a single person. There is no place like it in New York State or New Jersey. I met with more success here than at any other place.

THE TROUTER'S OUTFIT.

HE rod for stream fishing should weigh from three to six ounces and measure in length from seven to nine feet. Split bamboo and lancewood are two of the best rod materials. If you cannot afford a good split bamboo do not buy a cheap one; choose a lancewood.

The line should be a small sized waterproofed silk one. The reel, a small common light rubber click, holding twenty-five or thirty-five yards.

The landing net, used to take the fish from the water after being hooked, should be made of cane with linen netting, and no metal about it. The handle should be about a foot long. Tie a string to the handle, tie the string to a button on your coat under your chin, and then toss the net over your back out of the way.

The creel, or fish basket, a willow one

about the size of a small hand satchel. This should have a leather strap, to be slung over the right shoulder, allowing the creel to rest on the left hip.

The hat should be a soft brown or gray felt with two-inch brim. This may be used as a cushion to sit down upon on rocks or in damp places.

The foot wear may be either gum boots, leather shoes, or rubber wading trousers. If the water is warm, wear leather shoes, and have nails put in the thick soles to keep your feet from slipping in swift water and on slimy stones. If you choose gum boots, see that they are of the light, thin, thigh-fitting sort and not the clumsy affairs with straps attached.

The fly book for use on the stream should have room for not more than a dozen flies, with pockets for leaders, silk cord, small shears, and other tools. A larger book for your general stock of flies and leaders may be left at your rural lodgings with your tackle box and other traps.

The leader, to which are attached the flies in use, should be of the finest quality

The Trouter's Outfit. 55

of single silk gut, and in length three feet. Three or four of these attached make a cast.

The coat and general clothing should be of a dead-grass, gray, or light brown color. Have plenty of pockets, and tie a string to nearly everything you carry in them; so you cannot lose them if they fall from your hands.

The flies—every known variety of trout fly, providing you order only those of the finest make.

Do not undertake to go trouting stintingly equipped, which is not saying that you are to dress and act like a circus clown. But you must be properly outfitted. Good carpenters make good houses, but their work is better and more pleasant if they have good tools.

The tyro who is not fortunate enough to have the friendship of a practical fisherman to whom he may apply for advice should read the various sportsman's publications—*Forest and Stream, Shooting and Fishing, American Field, Outing, Recreation, Amateur Sportsman, Field and Stream, Sports Afield, The Sportsman's*

Magazine, and *Woodcraft,* and the works on angling and ichthyology by Izaak Walton, Frank Forester, Seth Green, Charles Hallock, Wm. C. Harris, Thaddeus Norris, Genio C. Scott, Fred. Mather, Robert Roosevelt, G. Brown Goode, Kit Clarke, Dr. Jas. A. Henshall, and John Harrington Keene, and make a study of the catalogues of the better class of sporting-goods houses.

LITTLE CASTS.

UP AND DOWN STREAM.—English anglers sometimes wade up a stream and some anglers in this country, in order to be English, or foolish, affect the same ridiculous proceeding. Still there is *some* reason in this manner of wading on the part of the old country's anglers, because where they practice it the water is quiet and not altogether shallow. Here, where our trout streams are rapid and foaming as they rush along, it is simply out of the question to wade up them. The walking is bad, you become wet, the fish see you, your flies drift toward you, your line is slack all the time and the flies sink too often, and altogether you spoil the chances of creeling whatever may be takable in the water. On still, barely-flowing, deep waters, a line may be cast in any direction.

✱

HOW TO CARRY THE ROD.—Joint your rod only when you reach the place for angling, and take it apart again when you are ready to leave the water for camp, unless the camp is on the edge of the lake or stream where you fish. When fishing along thickly-wooded banks, carry the rod in front of you, tip first; never pull it after you.

Fasten the hook on one of the reel bars, and then thrust the rod's tip through the branches or shrubbery ahead of you when you move along, casting here and there. This is not necessary when one only moves a step or two, for then, if there be open space, the rod and line may be held clear of the underbrush and branches. In all cases keep the rod ahead of you.

⁎

IN SPITE OF "PUCK" AND "JUDGE."—That old, faded yarn of the inexperienced, to the effect that the bent-pin-fishing country boy can catch more trout than the properly equipped angler is again in vogue, and the experienced rodsters who read it are again bubbling over with wrathful indignation. No impracticable boy, whether he be of the country or of the city, can excel the correctly rigged, careful fisherman. The bent-pin youth of the farm may outfish the unskillful, showy tyro from the city, but to compete with the scientific angler he would stand about the same chance of outfishing the expert as a cow would stand fishing alongside of a mink.

⁎

COLORS OF TROUT.—The color of a trout's back depends on the color of the bottom of the river, but the trout which grow rapidly differ greatly in spots and color from those which grow slowly and thrive badly, and a middle-aged trout differs in color from an aged trout. Speaking generally, the young, healthy, fast-grow-ing fish will have silvery sides, white belly, and plenty of well-defined spots. The poorly fed fish will have few or no spots, a drab belly, and muddy-yellow sides. The old trout will be particularly lank and large-headed.

****

TROUT IN CAPTIVITY.—Trout in artificial ponds should be fed three or four times a week in the winter time. The food should be cast in the warmest part of the day. There is no natural food in artificial ponds, and feeding is necessary in order to keep the big fish from eating their small companions. In natural trout ponds fed by springs so much care need not be exercised in winter. Air holes need not be cut in any ice that may form, as the springs afford a proper temperature, and but little food, if any, need be given the fish.

****

NO GREED.—I don't care if the fish that I catch weigh only a pound, no matter what the species may be. My tackle is light, fine, and properly rigged, and with it, in taking big fish or half-pound and pound fish, I have just as much sport as the man who uses heavy, coarse, ill-kept tackle on bigger game alone. The woodcock—the king of game birds—is bagged with No. 10 shot, but the sport of taking him is quite as great as the shooting of fowl ten times his size.

****

TRANSPORTING TROUT.—To bring your fish home, first clean them carefully, taking pains to remove that little dark blood streak along the backbone. Then, after wiping them dry, pack them in ferns and be careful to keep them separate and free from ice. Never send your fish home by express; take them with you. A box cannot be checked, therefore an old packing trunk is a handy thing. In this you can also put away your coarse outfit, such as wading boots, oil skins, and landing net.

ANGLER VS. POTSTER.—Trout in the creel or no trout in the creel, the truly gentle angler never complains of poor sport if there be trout in the water he fishes, if the weather be pleasant and the scenery fair. Some anglers—or rather pot fishermen—judge their day by the actual slaughter of fish. The true rodster loves the pursuit and capture of the fish, the bright day and the beautiful natural surroundings equally well.

TROUT IN MOUNTAIN LAKES.—Mr. Edward Sawyer of the Gramercy Park ranch has studied the problem of raising trout in mountain lakes. Proximity to a slaughter-house is a necessary condition to success, he thinks. In an artificial lake, however perfect it may be, the fish want regular and very considerable supplies of animal food.

A-WHEEL TO THE STREAMS.—Mr. David Rivers writes me: "I ride my wheel to my favorite fishing grounds regularly in the summer time, but I carry no paraphernalia. My rod and tackle box are left at the fireside of a friendly innkeeper. I am careful to nicely clean my outfit after each day's sport. The wheel is excellent for such trips."

THE FINGERLING FISHER.—It is no extraordinary thing to see great big men with a creel full of trout, each not over the size of a lady's penknife. They fill their basket, have their picture taken, and write to friends in the city glowingly of the "hundred and fifty speckled beauties" they secured in one day's play.

LIFELIKE.—Don't simply drag the fly through the water. Work your wrist gently up and down; then the lure will look like a living insect and not a bunch of hair or feather. You can't use too light a rod along mountain streams nor let the fly fall too lightly.

AN IDEAL TIME.—The last two weeks in June—what better period for brook trout fishing in the rich flower-lined mountain streams? When does the wild shrub smell sweeter than now, the wind blow more balmily, the songbirds trill livelier, and the spotted trout bite better?

TO EXTRACT HOOKS.—To extract fish-hooks from your flesh or clothing, cut the leader free and push the hook on through, depressing the upper end so as to bring the point out as near as possible to where it went in. Don't try to pull the hook back over the barb.

TAME TROUT.—An English gentleman has two brook trout that take flies from his fingers, and that ring a little bell cord when they are hungry. They were taught this latter performance by having bits of food tied to the cord when it was first introduced.

VARIETY.—You can never carry too many trout flies on your trip. Fill your fly-book and stick them all over the crown of your hat besides. Trout do not like the same fly at all times any more than you are fond of feeding on one sort of meat.

LANDING THE TROUT.—The proper time to spend in landing a fish all depends upon the condition of your fishing ground. Lead your prize away from obstructions, keep the line taut, and do not nervously hurry the play. Take your time.

DESTROYING THE STREAMS.—Discourage the indiscriminate cutting down of trees. The destruction of forest land means the drying up of trout waters and the devastation of drinking water.

Little Casts.

KNOTS IN RODWOOD.—Don't switch a light rod sideways. The maker may have purposely put a knot to one side, and this would cause the rod to snap.

⁂

THE BUNGLER.—Yarns and bragging puffs by bungling would-be fishermen annoy the practical man and puzzle the earnest tyro. The record of honest sport is entertaining and instructive.

⁂

STRIKING AND HOOKING.—Nothing is more difficult to learn about fly fishing than the art of striking or hooking the game.

⁂

DISCRIMINATION.—Do not worry if the fish are small; reduce your tackle. A vest pocket watch keeps just as good time as a town-hall clock.

⁂

SPORTSMANSHIP.—Chivalry to his companion and humane treatment to the game he pursues are the true sportman's axioms.

⁂

TROUT DESTROYERS.—Eels are ruinous to trout. They eat trout spawn, and they should be removed from all trout waters.

⁂

WOODCRAFT.—A good, simple way to find a road or dwelling, if you are lost in the woods, is to follow down a stream.

MOTION OF THE FLY.—In clear, smooth water let the fly sink a little, then move it along with a quick motion.

FEEDING-TIME.—Fish are said to bite between the new moon and the first quarter, the best, or between the last quarter and the change.

CLUMSY LURES.—Most trout flies are too large, and they serve more to frighten the fish than lure it in many cases.

CONSTANCY.—The assiduous man among anglers is the fish getter.

BE CALM.—Don't hurry a big fish. Kill him as far from you as possible.

THE BEST OF THE APOSTLES—Peter, Andrew, James, and John—were fishermen.

YOUR SHADOW.—Never let your shadow fall upon the water when angling.

NATURALNESS.—In fly fishing the lure must always be in motion.

ANCIENT LESSONS.—Parts of the Old Testament teach fish catching with both seine and hooks.

THE FLY ROD'S VICTIM.

TACKLE TALKS.

ALL-TIME FLIES.—For the young angler who does not care to go into the study of artificial trout flies and their seasons I will give here a list that may be used at all times, during legal seasons, and on all waters: Alder, gray and green palmer, ginger palmer, March brown, Reuben Wood, professor, white miller, coachman, royal coachman, codun, scarlet ibis, dark coachman, brown and red palmer, grizzly king, queen of the water, king of the water, brown hen, and blackgnat. Early in the season use hooks from No. 6 to 8; later No. 8 to 12. Use the small ones on streams and the large ones on lakes and rough waters; and, as I have previously remarked, when the day is bright and where the water is clear, use the small patterns of plain colors; on dark days and in the evening, use the large bright flies.

KNIFE AND SHEARS.—A small pair of scissors attached to a string and fastened to the angler's coat are most useful companions along the stream. They are much more easily operated than a knife; they save time, and while one may do with them nearly all that can be done with the knife, they will render a service that cannot be obtained from the single blade. A knife should always be carried, nevertheless, and the proper one for the trout angler is that newly invented thing which requires no finger-nail work and which is made ready for service by a mere pressure of the thumb on the top of the handle.

TROUTING OUTFIT.—Here's a plain, practical reasonable-price outfit with no unnecessary items: A four-ounce lancewood fly rod, a common rubber click reel to hold twenty-five yards of fine water-proof silk line, a seventy-five-cent cane landing-net, small and with no metal on it, a seventy-five-cent creel, a dozen of the best made and highest priced assorted trout-flies, a pair of waders, and a dollar's worth of the finest and best made silk gut leaders.

ROD DRESSING.—To whip rings or guides on the rod use silk twist, drawing the final end through a few coils of the whipping by means of a loose loop. To revarnish, wipe off all grease stains, and dress lightly down with the best copal. To reblacken brasses, mix a little lamp-blacking with spirit varnish. Dress once or twice and let the dressing thoroughly dry before using the copal.

BUY YOUR TACKLE.—The old anglers tied their flies themselves, and, in fact, made all their rods and tackle, save, perhaps, lines. To-day few anglers think of tying flies or preparing any tackle, owing to the expertness and moderate terms on the part of dealers. It is much cheaper to buy tackle outright as it is to buy gun shells ready loaded.

TO REMOVE A FERRULE.—Hold it over the flame of a spirit lamp or any flame until the cement is softened. If it has been pinned on, take a large needle, break it off squarely, put it on the pin, and strike just hard enough to set the pin below the ferrule, then warm and remove.

DYED FEATHERS.—Some say that no dyed feathers should be used in tying flies. We have always found dyed feathers practicable.—*London Rod and Gun.* But the fact remains, nevertheless, that all dyed feathers will fade to a damaging extent.

THE JOINTS.—If your rod joints go together harshly or do not come apart with ease, oil them lightly. See that no sand or any dirt gets in the ferrules. To take the joints apart easily when they are tightly set, gently warm the metal.

RUBBER BANDS.—Little rubber bands are practical items of a sportsman's outfit. One real service they render is in holding the fly rod joints together when you travel through the woods after your day's fishing.

***

CORK HANDLE.—To avoid blisters on the hand, have the handle of your rod covered with cork instead of cane, twine, or rubber. It will prevent the hand from slipping, is pleasant to the touch, and very light in weight.

***

SMOOTH FERRULES.—Before jointing your rod, oil the male ferrules with vaseline, or by rubbing them on the back of your neck. This will prevent the joints from becoming tight after the day's sport.

***

VEGETABLE LURES.—Bearded seed of the wild oat has been successfully used as artificial flies in fishing for brook trout, and bass have struck savagely at a silvery willow leaf flailed upon the water.

***

TO CARRY FLIES.—Do not use your big fly book when wading. Put a half-dozen killing patterns in your hatband, and a dozen more in a little book that will not bulge out your pocket.

***

BE PARTICULAR.—The finer the tackle the fairer the sport.

CARE OF THE ROD.—See that your rod-case is thoroughly dry before you put your rod in it, and always tie the case-strings loosely or you will have bent tips and joints.

POSITION OF REEL.—The reel of a bait-rod should be on the top side of the rod, in front of the handle; that of a fly rod on the under side below the handle.

EARLY-SEASON FLIES.—Dark stone, codun, alder, Bowman, black May, beauty, Ben Bent, blue bottle, hare's ear.

BORROWED THOUGHTS.

WHEN trout are taking the fly on the surface, and are not simply feeding on the larvæ as they swim upward, a brand new fly is more likely to catch a fish than one which has been a great deal used. I always use May-flies dressed on eyed hooks, have a goodly supply, and when one gets so wet as to necessitate a considerable amount of labor in the drying of it, off it comes, and is stuck in my cap to dry at its leisure. Of course it is rather wasting to the cast—this frequent changing flies—and no little trouble to those whose fingers are all thumbs, and whose eyesight is becoming dim, but it is far less trouble to change the fly than to dry it when thoroughly soaked.—*London Fishing Gazette.*

When the learner becomes accustomed to handling his rod, he must try to perfect himself in two matters of great importance—accuracy and delicacy. Place a small piece of paper fifteen or twenty feet away, and aim at making the knot in the end of the line fall easily and quietly upon it. Your efforts will be aided if you will raise the point of the rod a trifle just as the forward impulse of the line is spent, and the line itself is straightened in the air for an instant in front. This is a novel kind of target shooting, but its usefulness will be realized when the angler finds it necessary to drop his flies lightly just over the head of some wary trout.—RIPLEY HITCHCOCK.

Reader, did you ever throw the fly to tempt the silvery denizen of the lake or river to his destruction? Have you watched him, as it skimmed like a living insect along the surface, dart from his hiding-place and rush upon the tempting but deceitful morsel? Have you noticed his astonishment when he found the hook was in his jaw? Have you watched him as he bent your slender rod "like a reed shaken by the wind," in his efforts to free himself, and then have you reeled him to your hand and deposited him in your basket as the spoil of your right arm? If you have not, leave the dull, monotonous, everyday things around you and try it.—S. S. HAMMOND.

There is much diversity of opinion about the manner of fishing, whether up or down the stream. The great majority of anglers, both in Europe and this country, favor the latter method, and very few the former.—JOHN J. BROWN.

Lightning Source UK Ltd.
Milton Keynes UK
UKOW051423090112

185015UK00001B/112/A